Make It HAPPEN!

"Big Boy" Wills

CARTOONIST

RYAN HUME

Lightswitch
LEARNING

150 East 52nd Street, Suite 32002
New York, NY 10022
www.lightswitchlearning.com

Educators and Librarians, for a variety of teaching resources, visit www.lightswitchlearning.com

Library of Congress Cataloging-in-Publication Data is available upon request.
Library of Congress Catalog Card Number pending

ISBN: 978-1-68265-577-1
ISBN: 1-68265-577-6

"Big Boy" Wills by Ryan Hume

Edited by Lauren Dupuis-Perez
Book design by Sara Radka
The text of this book is set in Neuton Regular.

Printed in China

Image Credits

Cover: Newscom, Xinhua/Liang Xu
Page 1: See credits for cover
Page 4: Getty Images, arabianEye RF
Page 5: (top) Alamy; (middle) Getty Images, Aurora Open; (bottom) Getty Images
Page 6: Alamy
Page 7: Getty Images
Page 8: Newscom, Erich Schlegel/ZUMAPRESS
Page 9: Getty Images, iStockphoto
Page 10: Getty Images, Aurora Open
Page 11: Getty Images, iStockphoto
Page 12: Newscom, Erich Schlegel/ZUMAPRESS
Page 13: Getty Images

Page 14: Getty Images; iStockphoto
Page 15: Getty Images, Blend Images
Page 16: Newscom
Page 17: Getty Images, Hero Images
Page 18: Getty Images
Page 19: Getty Images
Page 20: Newscom, Erich Schlegel/ZUMAPRESS
Page 22: Newscom, Xinhua/Liang Xu
Page 23: Newscom, Xinhua/Liang Xu
Page 24: Getty Images
Page 25: Getty Images, iStockphoto

"I'm just a happy guy at heart."

Clarence "Big Boy" Wills Jr.

· · ·

Make It! HAPPEN!

Before Reading

Think about your own goals. Do you want to play soccer or write stories or make music? All of these activities take time and practice.

During Reading

During reading, keep an eye out for the highlighted vocab words. While learning about Big Boy's story, pay attention to how he got to where he is today. What **skills** has he shown that have helped his **career**? In each chapter, the Make It Happen! activity will help you, too, build skills to reach your own goals.

After Reading

Look in the back of the book for questions and activities to help you think about Big Boy's story. Share these with a friend, parent, or teacher. Also, talk about the skills you need to reach your goals.

skill: the ability to do something that comes from training, experience, or practice
career: a job that someone does for a long time

Contents

Early Life

Big Boy's family always supported him and surrounded him with love. By the time he was eight years old, Big Boy had a brother and four sisters.

Clarence Wills Jr. is from a close, loving family in New York City. When he was a baby, his older sister gave him the nickname "Big Boy." He had huge cheeks and big hair. His family still calls him that today.

The Wills family includes Big Boy's mother and his three sisters and brother.

Big Boy was a curious kid. The Wills family kept a library in their home. Big Boy would spend hours looking at books, touching each page. He would draw on blank pages. But Big Boy was not like other kids. He didn't respond to his name. He didn't laugh and play with people. At six years old, he was **diagnosed** with autism.

Autism is a medical condition. It changes how people **interact** with the world. Often, they are not good at talking. They might have trouble making friends. But Big Boy loved art. He became a cartoonist. Now he interacts with the world through his cartoons.

diagnose: to recognize a disease or illness by examining someone
interact: to talk or do things with other people

An Interest in Art

Big Boy comes from a supportive family. They helped him achieve **self-expression** through his art. His dad, Clarence, was a fireman. His mom, Ruth, was a stay-at-home mom.

Cheryl and Big Boy are close in age. They have a special bond that started when they were both just babies.

Even after being diagnosed with autism, Big Boy's life didn't change very much at home. "I didn't allow my children to be treated differently," his mom said. "And I certainly didn't treat them different [sic]." The family never left Big Boy out of things. "We didn't treat him like a special kid," his sister Cheryl said. "In all honesty, we didn't know what autism was anyway. He was fully included in everything we did. Birthdays, holidays, everything." His mom added, "If Big Boy wasn't invited, no one went."

self-expression: sharing your thoughts or feelings especially through artistic activities

Big Boy's family supported his love of books. This soon turned into an interest in art. Art became a way for Big Boy to express himself. His family taught him to read and write. They also helped him learn **self-control**, which can be hard for people with autism.

self-control: to have power over your feelings or actions

Make It HAPPEN!

Respect Differences

At some point in your school or job, you will have to talk to people who may not agree with you. Use your **critical thinking** skills and practice with a friend.

- Find a topic that you do not agree on and discuss it.
- Focus on the other person and listen carefully. This will help you understand them better.
- When you talk, take as much time as you need to get your point across.
- Explain why you feel the way you do. Avoid rude language. Talk to them as if they are a teacher or a parent.

How did it go? Ask your friend how they felt about your talk. Were you able to disagree with each other and still listen to what your friend had to say?

critical thinking: analysis of an issue in order to form an opinion

First Steps of the Journey

Cartoons inspired Big Boy to create his own art.

As a child, Big Boy loved cartoons. "He watched them differently than we watched them," said Cheryl. "We could watch them casually. But he was [very] focused and would not even turn his head from the TV when the cartoons were on."

Lardball, Super Stretch, and Pete Pretzel are some of of Big Boy's cartoons.

Then, Big Boy started teaching himself to draw. He created the characters he saw on the TV screen. He drew Woody Woodpecker, Bugs Bunny, and Popeye the Sailor Man. Big Boy was **dedicated** to his drawing. He drew the characters over and over again. Watching cartoons **inspired** Big Boy to become an artist. Practicing made Big Boy a better artist.

dedicated: having very strong support for or loyalty to a person, group, cause, or activity
inspire: to make someone want to do something

Big Boy "was trying to express this creative spark in him," Cheryl said. Soon, Big Boy had pencils, crayons, and a notebook with him all the time.

Artistic Activities

Big Boy's imagination started to grow. He began drawing for hours each day. Soon, Big Boy was also coming up with his own characters. "For most of my life, I have been creating cartoon characters," Big Boy said. "One day, I hope to be like the great Charles Schultz, who created the all-time favorite *Peanuts* characters. Snoopy was my favorite when I was a kid."

Big Boy has created hundreds of new characters. These include Donny Dwarf, Elmer Elf, and Gandalf Gnome. "He made his own friends in cartoons," Big Boy's mom said. "Other than his sisters and his brother, the cartoons became his lifelong friends."

Donny Dwarf, Elmer Elf, and Gandalf Gnome

When Big Boy feels inspired, he'll draw a **sketch** of his ideas on a pad of paper. Then a cartoon will come to life. These artistic activities are a large part of Big Boy's life. He carries a pad and pencil everywhere he goes. He could draw a cartoon at any time. Even in the car!

sketch: a quick, rough drawing that shows the main features of an object or scene

Make It HAPPEN! Keep a Sketchbook

Learning a new skill takes a lot of practice. Do you want to learn to draw? Keeping a sketchbook can help.

- Pick out a sketchbook. It should be small enough to fit in your backpack.
- Take the **initiative** to draw every day, even if it's only for a few minutes.
- Try different art tools. Use crayons, colored pencils, pens, or pencils.
- Look for ideas everywhere you go. You can draw what you see in real life. Or you can use your imagination.
- Find something you like to draw. Draw it over and over, like Big Boy did with his cartoon characters.

initiative: the determination to learn new things on your own; the ability to get things done

After a few weeks, look back at your earlier work. Has your drawing improved? How can you continue to improve?

Overcoming Obstacles

Big Boy begins all of his drawings with pencil first.

Like many people with autism, Big Boy has a hard time talking to others. He didn't start speaking in sentences until he was 12 years old. This made it hard for him to explain himself. His mom and **siblings** could understand him. But sometimes other people were mean to him because he couldn't express himself.

Big Red

Big Boy went to a school for students with **special needs**. The school supported him. But Big Boy didn't do well in art classes. "They wanted to tell him how to draw. And he already knew how to draw what he wanted to draw," his mom said. Sometimes artists are **innovative**. They don't do well with regular teaching. "It was like, in one ear [and] out the other," Cheryl said. "They wanted him to paint flowers. He didn't want to paint flowers. He wanted to create his characters."

sibling: a brother or sister
special needs: mental, emotional, or physical problems in a child that require a special setting for education
innovative: having new ideas about how something can be done

Some kids are inspired by what they see and read in books.

A Safe Space

During his youth, Big Boy received support from his family and his school. Because he was different than the other kids, Big Boy was **bullied**. Other kids would make fun of him and call him names. His sister Cheryl always protected him. His family made sure that he had room to play where other kids didn't bother him.

Safe spaces are important for people with autism. A safe space is somewhere people feel they can be themselves without being bullied. It can be their home, a special group, or even just a quiet room. Art and drawing can also act as a sort of safe space. By allowing Big Boy to draw, the Wills family was forming a safe space around him.

bullied: to be frightened, hurt, or threatened by someone else

With a loving home and the help of his school, Big Boy started to feel more comfortable around other people. "[Big Boy's school] did a fantastic job on speech and everything else," his mom said. "He started [speaking in] complete sentences and they taught him how to express himself."

Make It HAPPEN! Become a Volunteer

You can help your community by becoming a **volunteer**. It is a great chance to show initiative and gain **leadership** skills. Here's how you can get started:

- Find an **organization** in your community. Choose one that works for something you feel strongly about, such as animals or people with special needs.

- Identify your skills and make a list of what tasks you would do best. Choose when and how often you would like to volunteer.

- Meet with a volunteer organizer. Treat the meeting like a job interview. Dress nicely, be respectful, and come with a list of questions to ask.

leadership: the power or ability to be in charge of other people
volunteer: a person who does work without getting paid to do it
organization: a company, business, or club that is formed for a particular purpose

What could you volunteer to do to help your community? What skills are needed to be a volunteer? How can you get others involved?

Teamwork

Cheryl and Big Boy continue to be an amazing team.

Big Boy has always been very close to his sister Cheryl. Cheryl is a well-known TV news reporter. In 2010, Cheryl and Big Boy were speakers at the International Sibling Conference in Connecticut. The event thanks people who help and support their siblings with **disabilities**.

Cheryl and Big Boy spoke at the International Sibling Conference.

During the event, Cheryl first spoke for a few minutes about growing up with Bog Boy. Then she introduced her brother. Everyone clapped loudly. With **confidence**, Big Boy said softly into the microphone, "Thank you. Good evening. My name is Clarence Wills and I am very happy to be here. I'm just a happy guy at heart. I have a pretty big family, as you can see. My older sister Cheryl is like my best friend. Naturally, we are just like peas and carrots. She loves my artwork and tells me that I am going to be a great artist someday."

disability: a condition that damages or limits a person's physical or mental skills
confidence: a feeling or belief that you can do something well or succeed at something

Working Together

Big Boy and Cheryl **collaborate** to raise **awareness** about autism and other disabilities. They have spoken at many important events together. In 2010, Cheryl was asked to host a concert. Bands that have members with disabilities played at the event. "I told event planners that I wanted my brother Clarence to co-host with me," Cheryl wrote in the *Huffington Post*. "No him—no me."

Later, they hosted a film festival in New York. They also hosted an important event for a group that works with children and adults with special needs. Big Boy and Cheryl make a great team. Big Boy helps Cheryl host these events. He brings a unique **perspective** and artistic talent. As a cartoonist, he often designs posters for the events, too.

Cheryl and Big Boy spoke at the Apollo Theater for a concert for people with special needs.

collaborate: to work with another person or group in order to achieve or do something
awareness: the knowledge that a situation, condition, or problem exists
perspective: a way of thinking about and understanding an issue

Cheryl and Big Boy also made a school workbook for kids. The workbook teaches students about people with disabilities. By collaborating, Big Boy and Cheryl are making a big difference in the world.

Make It! HAPPEN!

Improve Teamwork Skills

Teamwork is necessary in order to have success in life, at school, or in a career. You can practice becoming a better team member by putting together a presentation on autism. Collaborate with at least two other classmates.

- Work together to write an outline for your talk.
- Discuss questions any group member might have.
- Decide who will say what.
- Look over each other's notes.
- Give feedback. Good feedback includes both compliments and tips to improve.
- Give your presentation.

How did it go? Were you a helpful teammate?

DIZZY

CARRIE AARON

SKIPPER

HANK

BURRITO

BONEHEADS

DINGO

MELVIS

BAYWICK

BASIE JONES

ALI

STER   PEPPER

DOBY

ROXIE   T-BONE

KIBBY

PORSHIA MUFFET DANA

GATOR   KHAZZAM

"BONEHEADS"

© CLARENCE

Big Boy now has a very strong **presence** in his community. His artwork can be seen in several places in New York. Many centers for people with disabilities feature Big Boy's drawings. His cartoons are also hanging in local libraries. His art has even been shown at a large college in New York.

Big Boy also enters his art into contests. He won a contest to make a logo for a government program. The program helps New Yorkers with disabilities. Every year, it helps thousands of people find new jobs. This allows them to become more **independent**.

At the Sibling Conference, Big Boy met actor Chris Burke. Chris has Down syndrome, but that has not stopped him from achieving his dreams.

presence: a noticeable and effective influence
independent: not requiring or relying on other people for help or support

With his sister by his side, Big Boy continues to speak to people at events. He is working hard to bring more awareness to autism. By being so active, Big Boy is really making a difference. His art and speeches help others who have autism and other conditions.

When Big Boy and Cheryl spoke at the Apollo, the entire Wills family was there for support.

A Family Man

Big Boy, now 49 years old, is a thoughtful and caring person. He is always thinking about his family. He cares very much for his mother. He now lives with her. "Where, oh where, would any of us be without our dear mothers?" Big Boy said at the International Sibling Conference. "I don't know where I'd be without her."

Big Boy continues to spend most of his time each day drawing. These days, he draws personal birthday cards. He makes them for everyone who is close to him. His family has grown beyond his parents and siblings. He now has many brothers-in-law, nieces, and nephews. "He never forgets," said Cheryl. "He writes on the inside, 'A thousand congratulations.' And he knows exactly what age you are," she said.

Determination and practice have helped Big Boy succeed. But he thanks his family most of all. He said at the siblings conference, "They have always been there for me, and I will always be there for them."

determination: a quality that makes you continue trying to do or achieve something that is difficult

Make It HAPPEN! Create Birthday Cards

Showing kindness toward others is something people should do every day. Show the people in your life you care by making personalized birthday cards, like Big Boy does for his family.

- Make a list of important people in your life. Add their birthdays and sort them by month.
- Write down a personalized message for them inside of their card.
- Create a picture for the front of each card that you think the person will like.
- Start making your cards now, or save your list for when a birthday comes up.

Once you give someone a card, think about how it made you feel. Did they appreciate it more because it was made by you?

Defining Moments

Big Boy has come a long way during his life's journey. There have been many important moments that have led him to where he is today.

1972
Big Boy starts drawing. He scribbles on the blank pages of books in the family library.

1974
Big Boy is bullied by kids in his neighborhood.

1975
Big Boy continues to develop his self-expression through art. He begins to draw cartoon characters.

1985

Big Boy makes birthday cards for his family members.

1991

Big Boy's cartoons are displayed in art galleries in Long Island, New York.

2010

Big Boy begins speaking to people at important events. This raises awareness of autism and other disabilities.

2017

Big Boy creates original artwork at the Exceptional Artists Foundation event in Hempstead, New York.

Depth of Knowledge

1 What does it mean to collaborate with other people? Use the relationship between Big Boy and his sister Cheryl for ideas.

2 Summarize how Big Boy stays active in his community.

3 How have Big Boy's discipline and initiative helped him to become an artist?

4 Write a guide for how to create a cartoon or comic strip. What skills are needed and why?

5 What is your opinion on the best way to learn something new, such as drawing? Write about the best way to learn a new skill. Support your point of view with facts from the story.

Prepare an Art Portfolio

Collaborate with a team of classmates to create a group art portfolio. A portfolio is a collection of work. It shows the artist's talents. Artists use portfolios when applying for jobs or selling their art.

WHAT YOU NEED

- Artwork from school and home
- Art tools, such as colored pencils or markers
- Folder or binder

WHAT TO DO

1 Gather the artwork you have created for the Make It Happen! features in this book. You can also use artwork from school or home.

2 Have each member explain their pieces. What do they contribute to the portfolio?

3 Create a cover for the portfolio using a folder or binder. Get creative!

4 Then, decide what you could do with your portfolio. Are there potential jobs? Who might want to show your work?

5 Collaborate to prepare a presentation of your portfolio. Discuss the skills needed to be successful as an artist. Are those skills shown in your portfolio?

Glossary

awareness *(noun)* the knowledge that a situation, condition, or problem exists (pg. 20)

bullied *(verb)* to be frightened, hurt, or threatened by someone else (pg. 16)

career *(noun)* a job that someone does for a long time (pg. 4)

collaborate *(verb)* to work with another person or group in order to achieve or do something (pg. 20)

confidence *(noun)* a feeling or belief that you can do something well or succeed at something (pg. 19)

critical thinking *(noun)* analysis of an issue in order to form an opinion (pg. 9)

dedicated *(adjective)* having very strong support for or loyalty to a person, group, cause, or activity (pg. 11)

determination *(noun)* a quality that makes you continue trying to do or achieve something that is difficult (pg. 25)

diagnose *(verb)* to recognize a disease or illness by examining someone (pg. 7)

disability *(noun)* a condition that damages or limits a person's physical or mental skills (pg. 19)

independent *(adjective)* not requiring or relying on other people for help or support (pg. 23)

initiative *(noun)* the determination to learn new things on your own; the ability to get things done (pg. 13)

innovative *(adjective)* having new ideas about how something can be done (pg. 15)

inspire *(verb)* to make someone want to do something (pg. 11)

interact *(verb)* to talk or do things with other people (pg. 7)

leadership *(noun)* the power or ability to be in charge of other people (pg. 17)

organization *(noun)* a company, business, or club that is formed for a particular purpose (pg. 17

perspective *(noun)* a way of thinking about and understanding an issue (pg. 20)

presence *(noun)* a noticeable and effective influence (pg. 23)

self-control *(noun)* to have power over your feelings or actions (pg. 9)

self-expression *(noun)* sharing your thoughts or feelings especially through artistic activities (pg. 8)

sibling *(noun)* a brother or sister (pg. 15)

sketch *(noun)* a quick, rough drawing that shows the main features of an object or scene (pg. 13)

skill *(noun)* the ability to do something that comes from training, experience, or practice (pg. 4)

special needs *(noun)* mental, emotional, or physical problems in a child that require a special setting for education (pg. 15)

volunteer *(noun)* a person who does work without getting paid to do it (pg. 17)

Read More

Amara, Philip. *So, You Want to Be a Comic Book Artist?* The Ultimate Guide on How to Break into Comics! New York : Aladdin, 2012.

Brent Weissman, Elissa. *Our Story Begins: Your Favorite Authors and Illustrators Share Fun, Inspiring, and Occasionally Ridiculous Things They Wrote and Drew as Kids.* New York: Atheneum Books for Young Readers, 2017.

Gainer, Cindy. *I'm Like You, You're Like Me: A Book about Understanding and Appreciating Each Other.* Minneapolis, Minn.: Free Spirit Publishing, 2013.

Garbot, Dave. *Crazy, Zany Cartoon Characters.* Irvine, Calif.: Walter Foster Jr., 2015.

Verdick, Elizabeth and Elizabeth Reeve. *The Survival Guide for Kids with Autism Spectrum Disorders (and Their Parents).* Minneapolis, Minn.: Free Spirit Publishing, 2012.

Internet Links

http://www.abcya.com/animate.htm

http://www.wedrawanimals.com/how-to-draw-woody-woodpecker/

http://www.bigblogcomics.com/2014/10/bugs-and-co-via-don-gunn.html

http://www.cyh.com/HealthTopics/HealthTopicDetailsKids.aspx?p=335&np=287&id=2356

https://www.youtube.com/watch?v=mtRYKjucDHk

http://kidshealth.org/en/kids/autism.html

Bibliography

Cheryl Wills. "International Sibling Conference." *YouTube.* YouTube, 1 Sept. 2010. Web. 30 June 2017.

Kashinsky, Lisa. "Making safe spaces for children with autism." *Eagle-Tribune.* Eagle-Tribune, 10 Apr. 2016. Web. 30 June 2017.

"Signs of Autism." *National Autism Association RSS.* National Autism Association, 2017. Web. 30 June 2017.

Wills, Cheryl. "Siblings on the Frontlines for People With Disabilities." *The Huffington Post.* Oath, Inc., 25 Aug. 2010. Web. 30 June 2017.

Wills, Cheryl. *Die Free: a Heroic Family History.* Minneapolis: Hillcrest Media Group, 2011. Print.

Index